D1571491

To God Be The Glory!

By Karen R. Lueders

A Pedal Down Promotions

Publication

Manitowoc, Wisconsin

To God Be The Glory!

By Karen R. Lueders

Front and back cover design: Kathy Roehrig of Pedal Down Promotions.

ISBN-13: 978-1-798-94221-5

Published by Pedal Down Promotions
Manitowoc, Wisconsin
www.pedaldownpromo.com
920-323-7970

Contents

Dedication   8

My Foreword   9

Romans 15:13   10

The Garden of Grace   11

Holy Spirit, Light The Flame   12

God Speaks   13

Happy Birthday Throught 1-24-17   14

Giving For You, Honoring You   15

Lost Now Found   16

Sure, Secure Eternity   17

Pray, Everything I Do   18

Precious Promises   19

Help Me Become The Person, Back To You   20

Psalm 25   21

He's Made Me New   22

He's Made Me New, Hope & Faith   23

Today's A Gift For You   24

Take My Hand & Lead Me   25

Go! Work For Me   26

Living Water & Bread of Life   28

Living Water & Bread of Life, God's Comfort   29

Heaven's Gate   30

Sanctify Me, Shared Blessings   31

Psalm 1   32

My Father In Heaven   33

Romans 15:13   34

Forgive Me   35

Light Of My Day   37

Walk Daily In Grace   38

Perfect Peace   39

Contents

Glory, Honor & Praise, Guide My Day	40
Shades of Grace	41
Soaring Anew	42
Sometimes I Wonder	43
You Met Me At My Lowest	44
Heaven's Glory	45
Heaven's Glory, Sitting At His Feet	46
Tribute to Nancy	48
Jesus' Voice	50
Everything Comes From Him	52
Lead Me Today	53
Moments In Time	54
Pray Without Ceasing	56
Remind Me What Matters, Your Courage For Mine	57
Ephesians 3:14-21	58
My Savior	59
A Revelation	60
A Revelation, Love My Neighbor	61
Move Me Forward	62
Gifts of Love	63
Psalm 147:18, I'll Follow You	64
Take Myself	65
Placed In Christ	66
Life's Key, God's Forgiveness	67
A New Name	68
A Sunny Spot, His 'Healing Balm'	69
The Park Bench, A Reminder	70
A Reminder, A Reminder	71
By Faith Alone, Lost Now Found	72
Giving For You, What Are You Looking At?	73
The Power of Your Name	74

Contents

The "SON"   75

Be Mindful in Jesus   76

GOOD ROOTS   77

Your Servant Beverly   78

Wings of Hope   79

Wings of Faith, Serving You   80

Personal Guard, A Coffee Break   81

Be Kind, Keep Me On Your Path   82

Return and Repent, A Spring Poem   83

Spiritual Feast, Forgive Me   84

Grateful Thoughts & Good Attitudes   85

Beauty of Jesus, Fruits of the Spirit   86

Thank You, Redeemed   87

Be A Friend To All   88

Water For My Soul   89

Draw Near To God   90

Jesus - My Treasure, Eyes of Love   91

Investing Time & Energy, Your Hand of Might   92

Sharing Jesus, His Life For Mine   93

This Place of Grace, Listen!   94

Dream Come True   95

Your Way of Life   96

Dream With God   97

Move Forward In The New   98

Hospitality   99

Give Him Thanks   100

The Christmas Call   101

His Gift For You   103

Daily Prayers, Life's Lessons, Daily Thoughts   105

Dedication

This book of poetry
Is dedicated to:
God, who gave me this gift.

To my loving family,
God blessed me with the best!!
May you know daily
Christ's hope & love for you...

My wonderful husband Bill,
Who listened lovingly & intently
To each finished poem...

My spiritual mentors:
Beverly & Dorothy,
And to
Deb & all my "grandma friends"
At the nursing home...
Thanks for your love & encouragement!

And to my friend MaryAnn...
Thanks for your constant support
& unconditional love!

And...to my granddaughter, Natalie, for your
Rainbow & sun drawing.
You color my life with your love!

To God Be The Glory!

My Foreword

<u>To You, Dear Reader</u>
It is my prayer that you will see
God's Hope for YOU through my poetry.
And if you're in a bad place now —
God will see you thru! It's HIS solemn vow!

Please take your time
To read each line.
His Words speak, I know it's true —
Let the poems He gave me, speak to you.

Be still & know
He is YOUR God!!
He'll light your way
When clouds are gray.

May His SON then shine on you,
And may you see His rainbow too.
His promises of Hope & Love,
This day, given to you, from up above.

Karen Lueders

Thank you! God bless you!
To God Be The Glory!

"May the God of Hope
fill you with all joy & peace
as you trust in Him, so that you may
overflow with hope
by the power of the Holy Spirit."

Romans 15:13

The Garden of Grace

In the garden of grace,
Sin is erased.
He restores my soul
And makes it whole.

Forgiveness comes
And mercy's there;
And a sweet fragrance
Fills the air.

The garden of grace
Is a beautiful place.
He is the Sun
And a new life's begun.

Oh, in this place
There is no disgrace.
I only can see
His Love shining on me.

-Written 4-12-16

11

Holy Spirit, Light the Flame

Holy Spirit, light the flame,
Make Your Light shine brightly.
Holy Spirit, use me now
For You're the Lord Almighty.

Holy Spirit, cleanse my heart,
Sanctify my soul.
Recreate me with Your Life
And broken, make me whole.

Take away all doubt, despair,
From sin and shame release me.
Give me faith and joy and strength;
Your power can only move me.

Let me share Your Love with all
And the Hope You've given me.
I lift my voice to praise You now,
My soul's with You eternally.

-Written 7-1-16

A blessing: Pray your day in the Spirit's Way.

God Speaks

I want you just to "be",
I don't want you to "do",
I want you just to "see"
The One who truly loves you.

Come home to me, come home to stay.
Come trust in me and not your way.
Come learn of me and do my Will —
Come hear my voice, it says "Be still".

No greater love is there than mine,
It "calls you in" to love divine.
You're valued, precious and adored.
I died for you and I'm your Lord.

My child, you cannot earn my love,
It's free, a gift from me above.
Salvation's come to you today.
I AM the Truth, the Life, the Way.

-Written Thanksgiving morning
November 2016

My Happy Birthday Thought
1-24-17

Black clouds gathered, the storm came & it
hit hard.
After the storm, the sky became gray
Meaning there was a light shining
somewhere behind the gray clouds.
Gradually, the gray lifted & I felt the LIGHT
OF GOD'S PRESENCE on me.
It was the "Son."
God showed me a beautiful, double
rainbow.
I smiled because His promise was true for
me:
The "Son" made everything beautiful in its
time & I was doubly blessed.

Eccl. 3:11 – "He has made everything
beautiful in its time."

Giving For You

Help me focus more on You, Lord,
Thinking much less of myself,
Then as You give me blessings,
I'll give more to someone else.

Help me give up what I can
So my life for You I live —
Then trusting You with all I am,
I'll have more of my life to give.

Honoring You

You are the Lord of my life
And Savior of my soul —
You redeem my broken heart.
Today it is made whole.

You are Lord of my life
And Savior of my soul —
Thanks, praise, glory to Your Name!
I honor You! It is my goal.

-Written 2-13-17

Lost Now Found

God looks for us, then finds us,
And keeps us in His Care.
He comes to seek & save the lost
And shows us He is there.

So hear God's Voice, He's calling YOU –
You're forgiven of your sin.
He'll introduce you to His Love...
Once found, He'll work within.

Luke 19:10 – "The Son of Man came to seek & to save what was lost."

Sure, Secure Eternity

Lord of my life, You've given me
Your free gift of eternity.
You tell my soul that it is well.
Your Life has conquered sin & hell.

All doubt is gone & I'm set free
Of Satan's doubts accusing me.
You are the Life, the Truth, the Way,
Dark thoughts are gone, You light the day.

Satan cannot conquer me
In Jesus Christ I am set free.
I'll put Your armor on each day
To shield attacks that come my way.

All praise to You for saving me,
Not just my life but every day.
I give You thanks for teaching me,
With You, I'll spend eternity.

-Written 2-13-17

Pray

Help me pray to You today,
Throughout my day in every way.
Asking You to help me see
Your Love leading & guiding me.
Give me Wisdom from above
Then send me out in strength & love.

Everything I Do

Everything I do, Lord, let it be for You.
Everything I say, Lord, be my words
today.
Every thought I think, do not let it "stink."
Everywhere I go, Your Love help me show.

Who can use a "lift" today?
Who can use a smile?
Who needs Your encouragement?
Let me go the extra mile.

Let me Your compassion show
And Your kindness too,
Let Your Love work for me
In all I say & do.

-Written 2-16-17

Precious Promises

You have precious promises
For me to think about.
You give me precious promises
When Satan comes with doubt.

"Do not fear, You tell me
& do not be dismayed.
The Great I AM has chosen you,
His work to be displayed."

I know Your strength will help me.
You hold me in Your Hand.
Your righteousness is over me,
Your work is being planned.

I believe Your precious promises
Are for my life, for me.
I know You work things for Your good,
Your Word, I do believe.

-Written 2-17-17

Help Me Become The Person

Help me become the person
You want me to become,
Each day I pray, Lord Jesus,
In me, Your will be done.
Holy Spirit, do the work
That You would have me do.
With the "new life" You have given me,
May I honor & serve You.

-Written 2-26-17

Back To You

Sometimes I am distracted
By the busyness of day,
And demands of the moment
Often lead me, Lord, astray.
Worries, problems, fill my mind
And soon I can be "blue" -
Remind me of my blessings
And bring me back to You.

-Written 5-30-17

Psalm 25

Today's the day I sing for You
To praise You for the honor due!
Lord, I lift my soul to You
And give You thanks for You are true.

True to Your Word, I trust Your Love,
You give me music from above!
May all who hear to You draw near
And KNOW YOU as their Savior dear!

This poem was written
before a music presentation
at Good Shepherd, Plymouth, WI.
2-26-17

21

He's Made Me New

Lord, because of You, I can be "me,"
In Jesus Christ, I am set free.
Satan had his chains on me
To keep me down eternally.

Satan attacked my spirit cause
He wanted me to doubt God's Love.
He shot his arrows at my mind,
Full force he came to keep me "blind."

"You can't trust Jesus Christ," he said.
"Where is His help? He must be dead."
In discouragement, despair,
He told my mind, God can't be there.

Well, Satan, your words no longer stand
'Cause Jesus reached down & took my hand.
He picked me up, His grace to see,
And told me, "Come to Calvary."

"Look at me here, I died for you.
You are washed clean! I made you new!
I am your Savior, Lord, & Friend,
My Love for you will never end."

Continued

"Your sins & past are all forgiven,
I rose to give you the gift of heaven.
Satan, he's in bondage now,
I won the battle & threw him down!"

"Now run the race I have for you.
Say, 'He's alive! He loves you too.'
Go tell all they are set free…
He'll make you "new" like He's done for me."

-Written 2-26-17

Hope & Faith

Lord, You take my shame
And turn it into glory for Your Name.
All praise to You & honor too!
Show me how to work for You.

Today's a new day! Help me start
To share Your Hope within my heart.
Give me wisdom! Help me see
Your grace works faith inside of me.

-Written 2-27-17

Today's A Gift For You

Today's a gift to use for You,
Lord, show me what I am to do.
The Great I Am is over me,
Under His grace I am set free.

Free from Satan's doubts, despair,
With Jesus Christ, I'm meant to share
My day with those who need His Love,
The Lord will lead me from above.

Help me not to waste this day,
Give me Your Word to guide my way.
Send me Your Light so I can see
What path & doings You have for me.

-Written 2-27-17

Take My Hand
& Lead Me

Take my hand & lead me, Lord,
Thru the open door.
You closed the "window of my life,"
So I would love You more.

You set me on "The Rock" to stand
After my trips & falls,
You lifted me & gave me strength,
With You, I now stand tall.

You say, "Now come & follow me
Through this open door,
You have done life on your own,
It's gone! I now have more."

There's a plan, a purpose to live for You,
Lord, You show the Way to go —
For the Great I Am is over me,
His power & grace to show.

-Written 3-1-17

Go! Work For Me

"Come! Let's go!" You say to me,
"There's work to do. Come, follow me!
I'll lead you in the way to go.
Don't resist. I love you so."

"Fast for me & seek my face.
I say each day live under grace.
You were broken, now you're whole.
Be who you are! I've saved your soul!"

"Salvation's come to you today.
Get up! I'm with you all the way.
The Holy Spirit's in your heart.
Today's the day that you must start."

"A new beginning I have for you.
The Father's work is what you'll do.
My purpose, plans, you must pursue,
My Love will work inside of you."

"I AM the Way, the Truth, the Life.
I'll give you peace when you have strife,
I'll make you strong when you are weak,
The GREAT I AM works best when meek."

Continued

"All doubt is gone! Your faith saves you.
Step forward now! There's work to do.
Go share My hope in Jesus' Name,
Go tell My Love & bear no shame."

"Teach them what they need to hear.
Give them Life for they are dear.
Grace over sin, heaven for hell,
Truth over lies, the devil fell!"

Say: "Jesus' Love can set you free!
He died & rose so you can be
His child now & you can see,
He loves you thru eternity."

Amen! Amen! So shall it be!
I'll do the work You have for me.
I'll share Your Love & sing Your praise!
I'll honor You with all my days.

-Written 2-23-17

Living Water & Bread of Life

Why be downcast, O my soul?
Put your hope in God.
Why the sad face, O my spirit?
See the path your Savior trod.

My soul, you need the Living Water
Only God provides,
So drink here from the "Well of Life"
Or you shrivel up & die.

You're thirsty for His Love & Hope
So rest & take a drink!
This Water throws all doubts away,
Faith flows from it, so think!

Think of His Love for you, O soul!
You never are alone!
He lives! He's watching over you
And sits upon His throne.

The Water's from the throne to you
And the Bread of Life's nearby.
His Word is food for you, O soul,
Drink & eat this or you'll die.

Continued

Then He'll direct you with His Love -
Soul, He's what gives you life!
Praise your Savior & your God!
He raises you from strife!

The Living Water & Bread of Life
Gives joy, & peace, & rest.
Go! Drink & eat & talk with Him!
He waits & gives the best!

-Written 2-24-17

God's Comfort

Today when I feel lost & alone,
Remind me You're with me in my "heart's
home."
Whatever loss & trial I face,
You exchange comfort in its place.

Pain & sorrow bring sadness galore
But then You knock at our heart's door;
Reminding us we're not alone,
You bring love & comfort from Your throne.

Heaven's Gate

Thank You for dying on the cross for me,
Taking my sins & shame to Calvary.
You suffered to remove all of my guilt.
You conquered Satan so my soul can't wilt.

You gave Your life so I could have mine,
You shed Your blood, O Love divine!
I see You hanging on the cross for me,
I cry! You truly have set me free.

Satan has no hold on me
And death was conquered mightily,
You hung Your head & it was done.
You fought hell's battle & You won.

When they put You in the grave —
You rose & lived, my soul to save!
You live on high, You reign above!
Heaven's gate is open by Your Love.

-Written 3-3-17

Sanctify Me

Sanctify me thru & thru,
You are faithful. You will do
The holy work inside of me;
So my whole spirit, soul & body,
Lives for Thee.
Amen!

-Written 3-13-17

Shared Blessings

Today, Lord, let me count my blessings
With Thanksgiving in my heart,
For You have cared for me, dear Lord,
And my day with You I'll start.
Let me accept Your blessings
And gifts with praise to Thee –
Help me share them now with others
Just as You first shared them with me.

-Written 5-30-17

Psalm 1

In this season of my life, Lord,
Let me meditate on You,
For when my way is darkened,
It's You who sees me thru.
Give me a stronger faith
And as You care for me,
May I care for others
With what You've given me.
And as I pray this psalm, Lord,
You've given me a reason
To plant myself, deep in Your Word
For You will "yield its fruit" in season.

-Written 6-15-17

My Father In Heaven

My Father in heaven, I need Your Love
As You look down from up above.
Your Name is holy, pure and true.
Help me, Lord, be more like You.
Your kingdom come to me today
And show the path to light my way.
The daily gifts You give to me
I thank You, Lord, on bended knee.
Forgive my wrongs! You've paid the price!
For me, Your Son was sacrificed.
Help me forgive hurts done to me
'Cause You suffered for mine at Calvary.
Keep me strong so I don't fall
Into the devil's evil call!
Deliver me from all his ways
To walk with You thru-out my days.
Your kingdom come, rule over me
In Power and Glory eternally.
Amen!

-Written 9-27-17

Based on the Lord's Prayer

Romans 15:13

Thank You, God, for hope,
And hope's found in believing;
Trusting in Your Spirit's power
For joy & peace receiving.

Overflow my heart, dear Lord,
With hope that comes from You.
Each day fill me with Your love
So joy & peace shine thru.

Believe & you'll have joy & peace
Whatever you go thru -
Trusting Him each waking day,
His hope will live in you.

-Written 4-29-17

Romans 15:13 – "May the God of hope fill you
with all joy & peace as you trust in Him,
so that you may overflow with hope
by the power of the Holy Spirit."

Forgive Me

Forgive my many sins, Lord,
In thought & word & deed.
It was all my "dirty" sins, Lord,
That brought Your Son to bleed.

Jesus, You died upon the cross
And suffered for my sake.
You were innocent, holy, perfect,
And my place You did take.

I'm sorry, Lord, for still doing wrong,
For I see You die for me –
It took Your blood to save my soul,
Your Love endured such agony!

When I see You on that cross,
My eyes fill-up with tears,
I know You suffered for all the wrong,
I did thru-out my years.

I am humbled & sad, when I see
Your Love pierced & nailed for me.
I am thankful, Jesus, You saved my soul –
When You hung at Calvary.

Continued

I am sad, yet glad at the same time,
Sad – You beared the pain,
But tears are shed for gladness too,
For with You in heaven I'll reign.

Forgive me, Lord, for ever wanting
Sin instead of You.
I love You, Lord, make me never forget
What I put You thru.

I praise & thank You in my heart.
Oh, Love that died for me!
Amazing Grace! You saved my soul!
Jesus! Love's gift thru eternity!

-Written 3-7-17

Light Of My Day

Light of my day,
Change my way –
Make me obey
Your will today.

Give me a new direction
And new love,
Filled with Your power
From above.

I am wrong
And You are right,
Fill me with
Your holy light.

Send me forth
Your will to do,
Give me zeal
And grace from You.

-Written 4-21-17

Walk Daily In Grace

This morning, Lord, I seek Your face,
You say to me, "Walk in My grace."
I need to live Your Word each day.
It lifts, encourages, shows the way.

You give me grace for work to do,
You call me to walk close to You.
Your grace provides all I need,
Your Word speaks to my heart indeed.

I listen to Your Voice & hear
Grace is power & You are near,
To accomplish all I need to do,
So today – Lord, let me walk with You.

-Written 4-28-17

Perfect Peace

When the storm is raging around me, Lord,
Help me keep my eyes on You,
For wind and fears toss me about
But You will see me through.

Help me to hear the Words You speak
When the rain is pouring down,
For I know You calm the wind and sea,
Your peace and love abound.

Jesus, teach me to draw peace from You
And calm the storms of life,
For trials blow so often, Lord,
Around me, so much strife.

So I'll keep You at the center, Lord,
When the wind swirls me around,
Then peace and stillness of my soul
Will help me stay aground.

Abide with Him in every trial
And whatever comes your way,
He'll give you peace and calm your heart
As you trust Him day by day.

-Written 5-12-17

*Isaiah 26:3 – "You will keep in perfect peace
whose mind is stayed on You,
because he trusts in You."*

Glory, Honor & Praise

Glory, Honor & Praise to the Lamb
That was slain –
My soul lives with You
In paradise to reign!!

-Written 4-11-17

Guide My Day

Help me with my day
And teach me how to pray.
What should I do to love and serve You?
When resistance sets in –
Teach me to begin!
Guide my day only in Your Way.
In Jesus' Name I pray… Amen.

Shades of Grace

'Fifty Shades of Gray',
A bestseller on the book list,
Was a must-read by so many
Telling sexual fantasies wished.

I thought about how many minds
Wondered through the door,
As Satan led them down the path
Of fantasies galore.

I stopped, considered a different book
And how it's changed my life –
God's Word, the Bible, a "must-read"
Told me to be a godly wife.

I've learned life's hard lessons,
Years of wanting and seeking more –
My mind and life were fantasy
And God had so much more in store.

Choices come and choices go
And I must tell you this,
God's Word, His path now for my life,
Is on my MUST READ list.

Instead of wanting 'Shades of Gray',
My time with God I'm spending.
For my Savior gives me 'Shades of Grace,'
Gifts of His Love unending.

-Written 5-30-17

Soaring Anew

Lord, thank You for refueling me
When I feel overwhelmed –
When darkness covers my mind's thoughts,
Shed Your Light on them.
I am on a crooked path,
But You can make it straight.
With Your Light on each step I walk,
You'll lead me to the gate.
Silence is a discipline and when I'm feeling
weak-
You wisely teach that there are times
To be silent and to speak;
To rest and know that You are God,
To surrender my heart to You,
Refuels, renews me with Your strength,
Where I can soar anew.

-Written 6-14-17

Ps. 46:10 – "Be still and know that I am God."
Eccl. 3:7b – "There's a time to be silent and a
time to speak."
Is. 40:31 – "But those who hope in the Lord will
renew their strength.
They will soar on wings like eagles;
They will run and not grow weary, they will
walk and not be faint."

Sometimes I Wonder

Lord, sometimes I wonder,
How am I to pray?
In my heart You answer me,
"Just talk to me through-out your day".

Lord, sometimes I wonder,
What am I to do?
"Just look to me and say with faith,
I need wisdom so I'll trust You."

Lord, sometimes I wonder,
Where am I to go?
"I'll lead the way, just follow Me,
In My time, You'll know".

Lord, sometimes I wonder,
What am I doing here?
"My Love created you for Me
So to Me draw near."

Lord, sometimes I wonder,
What's life all about?
"Give your life to me, dear one,
Trust and do not doubt."

Your Love, O Lord, envelops me
And shows me what I am to see.
I see You die and live for me –
You love me through eternity.

You take my questions, all of them,
And give me faith. I say, Amen.

-Written 8-7-17

43

You Met Me
At My Lowest

You met me at my lowest
So I would know You better.
You have taught me I can trust You
Even in the darkest weather.

You held me up when I was weak,
When I couldn't do a thing.
You spoke Your music to my soul
And taught my heart to sing!

You took me through hard places,
It was not my will to go —
It was Your plan to teach me,
Alone with You, my faith would grow.

I never thought I would say thanks
For the trouble that came my way,
But thank You for Your saving grace,
I stand in faith today.

So, use me as You will, Lord,
I'll never be the same…
You've refined me through the fire
To glorify Your Name!

-Written 8-29-17

Phil.2:13 – "For it is God who works in you to will & to act according to His good purpose."

Heaven's Glory

Today the winds are blowing hard,
As the last days of summer are here.
Outside my window a lone daisy stands –
It's beauty, so lovely & clear.

Entranced, I watch it dance & sway,
Its delicate petals full bloom;
So tall & stately, yet weak & frail –
I watch it from my room.

Autumn's here now & in my heart
I know it will be gone,
But spring will bring it back again –
Again, full bloom & strong.

God's eyes see my beauty too,
Like the daisy all alone.
He's watching me from up above
As He sits upon His throne.

He sees me sway & being bent
In the golden years of life.
He says to me, "Do not fear!
I AM with you through the strife."

Continued

"I take care of the flowers –
They're gone, they are no more;
But you will know the joys of heaven
And what I have in store."

"So rest, my child, you're in my care,
Don't try, just trust in me!
The simple joys I give you,
Like the daisy; from heaven's majesty."

"Well done, good & faithful one!
Your soul is saved in me!
My Love & Beauty is here for you!
Heaven waits! My glory you'll see!!"

-Written 9-15-17
For my 95-year-old friend Dorothy,
who resides at a nursing home.

Sitting At His Feet

Today You teach me fellowship
And that it must be chosen –
Spending time with You, my Lord,
Keeps my heart from being "frozen."

So I will sit at Jesus' feet
Like Mary did long ago,
While Martha ran around and served,
Running to and fro.

Continued

Mary's love for Jesus
Moved her to humbly sit.
She listened, learned what Jesus said
And then her heart was lit.

Her heart lit-up as Jesus spoke
His Word and all His Ways –
He taught Mary to apply His Truths;
This guided her all her days.

He still teaches us today,
To grow in love for Him,
But we need to sit and listen,
For His Word to work within.

So open your heart this morning
Before you start your day.
This will strengthen you and help you trust
Whatever comes your way.

Spending time at Jesus' feet
Will give you peace above,
Then you'll get up and serve His Way
In fellowship and love.

-Written 10-2-17

Tribute to Nancy

My friend just passed away today
Which makes me very sad.
I'm glad I saw her Thursday,
When our hearts were very glad.

I kissed her on the forehead
As I walked into the room.
I said, "I love you, Nancy,"
And she said she loved me too.

She was sitting in her wheelchair,
Smiling, and her voice was very strong.
She looked cute in her ponytail,
Looking like nothing could be wrong.

She called me many times each week
Just to say hello –
Her sister's voice I heard just now
To say she's gone for sure.

She blessed my heart so many times,
She was a true friend who cared.
Through the years, the memories now,
Are ones her & I have shared.

Continued

I always will remember her
Short, little hi.
And now my friend, I say with tears,
It's time to say goodbye.

You taught me to have patience
And to take the time indeed,
To call, to care, to spend the time
'Cause we don't know when they'll leave.

But I will see you once again –
'Cause I know you've prayed for me
So God, take care of Nancy –
Till her 'welcome smile' in heaven I see."

Bless you, girlfriend!
I love you!!
Karen 10-1-17

Jesus' Voice

Satan wants to keep us down
In struggles and despair –
He knows time spent in thought of "us",
Will really lead nowhere.

In misery, self-pity, he destructs
Our every thought.
He tells so much discouragement,
We don't pray as we ought.

He knows that when we pray to Christ
He's doomed and cannot win,
So my prayer now goes to heaven
To forgive me of my sin.

Sins won for us at Calvary
Where it's Jesus voice we hear. –
"Forgive them Father" shows His Love
And says to me draw near.

So today I'll listen to You, my Lord,
Thoughts of Your Love, Your Power,
And with Your strength and with Your help,
Today I will not cower.

Continued

So, get behind me, Satan!
I'm listening to you no more!
It's Jesus who is leading me –
On eagles' wings I'll soar!!

Be careful who's voice you're listening to,
As you begin your day –
The Holy Spirit is here to help
When you begin to pray.

-Written 10-16-17

Everything Comes From Him

I can do nothing on my own –
Everything comes from Him.
So, God, forgive my prideful heart,
It's You that works within.

Many times I see things done
And I want all the credit,
Then You remind me who You are
And I should not forget it!

Forgive my pride and arrogance
And thinking of myself –
'Cause You, Lord, want to teach Your Power
Over my ignorance.

I've lived life only for myself,
Not what You've planned for me!
Forgive me, I surrender all –
It's Your Will, I want to see.

So use me, take me, no longer my own,
I humbly bow before Thee,
With Your Power working inside my heart,
My doings will show Your Glory.

-Written 10-19-17

Lead Me Today

Today's another day You give me,
Teach me not to waste it.
I need Your leading & Your Love
For me to truly live it.

Who should I help? Who should I call?
Who needs a lift from You?
Bring to mind whom I should serve
And then, Lord, help me do it!

For time marches on so fast,
I've wasted many days!
Forgive me, help me share Your Love,
Your heart and all Your Ways.

So today I start my day with prayer,
And surrender my heart to You.
Help me serve in Your Name,
And lead the whole day through.

-Written 10-19-17

Moments In Time

I used to sing 'One Moment In Time',
It was my favorite song –
In an early stage of my life
When I needed to belong.

Belong to social standing
And a step "above" the rest,
Where moments were an image
And I needed to impress.

Each life has its season
And lessons to be learned;
Through trials, set-backs, even blows,
In moments of concern.

We ask, 'Is life about my success,
High standings...the good I do'?
No! There's a true Teacher up above
Who's in charge of me and you!

My moments and days belong to Him,
They are not to be lived by me.
Hard lessons learned have come to this;
I get on bended knee.

Continued

54

I humbly bow before His Love
And this Love changes me —
To put Him first in my day;
Living moments for His Glory.

We have it backwards,
We put us first, when it really should be Him.
He has the plan for our life,
Believe…And His Spirit enters in.

For who can love me more than Him?
He creates me as His own.
I humbly work for Jesus now,
My King, who's on His throne.

Thank You, Lord, for this new season,
Serving others and showing You,
The God who graces my 'moments in time',
Has my life and wants yours too.

-Written 10-19-17

Pray Without Ceasing

God tells me in His Word
To pray now without ceasing,
So right now I'll give concerns to Him
'Cause these problems I'm releasing...

I give my worries, doubts to Him
'Cause each moment He wants to see
Me hand them over to His Love
So He can give His peace to me.

I'm learning, Lord, to talk to You
And ask You for Your help –
For You say, "Cast all Your cares on ME",
And take them off myself.

So I'll give You what is bothering me,
And trust Your answers, where and when -
I ask Your Will be done, O Lord,
Thanks for the blessing You will send.

-Written 11-5-17

1 Thes. 5:17(KJV) – "Pray without ceasing."
1 Peter 5:7 – "Cast all your cares on Him for He
cares for you."

Remind Me What Matters

Help me to build my life on things
That are eternal, Lord:
God's Love, God's grace, God's promises,
God's Son to be adored.
Remind me these are what truly matters
And not to focus on me.
For it's You, Lord Jesus Christ, that gives
God's gift of eternity.
So help me honor You, dear Lord,
With my prayers, & praise & service.
With thanks for all You've done for me,
It's You I want to worship.

-Written 5-10-17

Your Courage For Mine

I need courage along the way,
I need strength for each new day.
I trust You with each waking hour
To fill me with Your Spirit's Power.

Ephesians 3:14-21

I kneel before You, Father dear,
And ask in Jesus' Name draw near.
Glorious riches You give to me,
Surrendered to Your majesty.

You strengthen me in this hour,
My inner being has Your power –
You dwell within my heart thru faith.
I thank You for Your saving grace.

I am rooted in Christ's Love,
Give me wisdom from above,
To grasp how wide, long, high, & deep
This Love pours over my soul to keep.

Fill me with Love's fullness, Lord,
With Your Spirit working I rest assured -
You're able to do more than I ask,
Immeasurably more to work each task.

To You be Glory in the church!
In Jesus Christ You did the work
Of keeping generations strong –
To You, Loving Father, we belong!

-Written 11-14-17

Based on Apostle Paul's prayer to the Ephesians
-Ephesians 3:14-21

My Savior

You change my life & make me new
So I can live my life for You.

You send me Power from on high
To live in Truth before I die.

I am forgiven! I am set free!
Satan's chains are off of me.

You give more faith to truly see
My Savior rose in victory.

I yield to You all that I am.
I praise You, Savior, Lord & Friend.

Help me honor, serve You with my time,
Sharing the GIFT OF YOU, O Love Divine!

A Revelation

I hear You knocking on the door
And, Lord, please do come in!
I've lived life on my own too long,
A life of lust & sin!

I could not see, I was naked, blind —
Just doing my thing for "me".
I did not realize there was more,
Until I heard You knock for "me".

I thought I had life figured out
And I knew You, God, loved me.
But thru Your discipline & fire,
You made me "new" indeed.

I opened the door & You came in
To "clean me up" for You.
You told me to REPENT & then
Washed clean, I was made "new".

You covered all my shameful deeds
And white clothes You put on me,
Then healing salve touched with Your Love,
You gave new eyes to see.

Continued

Your Spirit now lives in my heart
'Cause I opened the door to You,
Surrendering all I am & have,
I live my life for You.

Rev. 3:19 – "Those whom I love I rebuke &
discipline. So be earnest, & repent.
Here I am! I stand at the door & knock. If
anyone hears my voice & opens the door,
I will come in & eat with him & he with me."

Love My Neighbor

Help me to love & serve
My neighbor as myself.
Send Your Love into my heart
To share Your peace & rest.

Calm their fears! Remove their tears!
And give them Love's assurance.
Let me share how much You care
So they can trust in Your reliance.

For times are hard & times can be
Suffering emotionally.
Let them see Your Love thru me
And lead them to You eternally.

Move Me Forward

Lord, keep me out of the "dry desert",
Where I think You've deserted me.
Move me in Your Spirit, Lord,
With Satan way behind me.

Speak to my heart & tell me
What I need to hear.
And then with Your hope & help,
I'll move forward with You near.

I cannot move without Your Love
And Your Spirit leading me.
I give You my frustrations, Lord,
Help me not to think of "me".

When I try to do things;
Myself & only on my own –
You remind me, "We" can do things
Altogether & be strong.

So today I'll trust You with my time
And look ahead with hope –
Giving You my heart & hands,
I know I now can cope.

For daily You take care of me
And I know I don't deserve You.
It's only when my faith's in You
That I can really serve You.
Continued

So make me diligent to act
And work faith in my heart –
Now, Holy Spirit, lead me forth,
With You, my day, I'll start.

Gifts of Love

Help me notice all the blessings
You have placed, Lord, in my life.
The beauty of fresh, fallen snow –
A wonderland of sight.

May I appreciate the little things
That brighten up each day –
An unexpected phone call from a
Friend who called today.

The morning sky in splendor –
Pink & purple gray,
Your majesty at work displayed
In waking up the day.

Every good & perfect gift
Comes from You above.
Thank You for reminding me –
Gifts of the moment are Your Gifts of Love!

Psalm 147:18

A Word from His mouth
Can melt any snow,
And when He speaks,
The wind surely blows.

God created the heavens
And earth to show,
The very breath of Him,
Makes the water flow.

Psalm 147:18 – "He sends His Word & melts them;
He stirs up His breezes, and the waters flow."

I'll Follow You

It's black & I don't know the way,
But I'll trust & listen to all You say.
You know the path to lead me on
And I know we now have just begun.

It's scary, Lord, not knowing where
You'll take me in the coming year,
But You lead & I trust You'll see me thru,
So take me, Lord, I'll follow You.

2018 New Year Poem

Take Myself

TAKE MYSELF…It belongs to YOU,
And show me what I am to do.

Lord, take ALL of me, each part,
Lead me with YOUR LOVING HEART.

Each day I'm meant to give my all
As I hear Your Spirit call.

The GREAT I AM has shown me "things"
Cannot replace 'His Eagle's Wings'.

Thank You, Lord, for saving ME,
Your Grace lives in me eternally!

My 65th Birthday Poem
To God Be The Glory!

Place In Christ

I am placed in Christ,
He surrounds me with His Love —
Above, before, behind, within,
Around; His Spirit from above.

I thank You, Lord, for helping me
To know Your Love is here,
Protecting me from evil darts
When Satan draws too near.

So place me center in Your care
And whatever comes my way —
I know in faith, Your Love shields me,
Each & every day.

Jesus Is Calling

Jesus is calling & waiting for You —
He wants to be with You, your whole day thru.
So remember, friend, take Him along,
He's singing over you, "Love's Sweet Song."

Life's Key

Life's Key is found in freedom
Offered by Christ on the cross.
It's freedom from a selfish life,
From sin & guilt & death.
It frees us for creative living
That the Spirit works within,
A life of loving service
Where eternal life begins.

God's Forgiveness

Today the snow falls gently down
And covers the ground in white,
Reminding me God's forgiveness comes –
Making all things new & bright.

Rev. 21:5 - "Behold! I make all things new..."

A New Name

Thank You for a New Name
You've given me in life –
To be called a Child of God...
Sinner to "New Life".

You didn't leave me, Lord,
Dying in my sin –
But picked me up & led me forth,
A new life to begin.

So now I know that when I die,
In heaven I will be –
And at the Name of Jesus,
I'll bow down on bended knee!

*Phil. 2:10 – "That at the Name of Jesus every
knee should bow, in heaven & on earth..."*

A Sunny Spot

When you are discouraged,
Find a sunny spot —
Let Jesus shine His Light on you,
For you're with Him or you're not.

For when we question or we doubt,
We forget His Love is there.
So sit! He'll shine His Light on you
And warm you in your chair!

And…Also, say a prayer!!

His 'Healing Balm'

Years ago when times were tough,
I walked along the lake.
I now think as I watched the waves,
It was my healing place.

Somedays the lake was, oh, so rough!
And somedays a peaceful calm —
And as the tide turns thru the years,
Jesus gives His "Healing Balm."

The Park Bench

I go to the park today & see
A bench to sit...Yay! It's there for me!
I take a break & sit awhile,
I think & then I have to smile.

There's "benches" along my path today,
Placed by someone who's trying to say,
Stop! Somebody saw beauty here.
Sit down & look! And it will be clear.

So give me the grace to pause awhile,
And then, like me, you'll have to smile.
God's creation & scenery I now can see,
Inspired by Him, God's majesty!

A Reminder

Never take your loved ones
For granted, that's for sure.
For each day is numbered
For all to endure.
So reach out to them
And let them know you care.
A reminder: Tomorrow they might
Not be there.

A Reminder

We have two ears & only one mouth,
So listen twice as much as you "spout";
Two arms & hands so don't forget,
There's one hand to give & one to get.

-Written 2-18-18

A Reminder

Do we see aggravations as inconveniences
As each day on earth we trod?
It may help to see them as reminders
That we need to draw near to God.

By Faith Alone

Noah had an extreme act of faith
When he built the ark under God's grace.
He was obedient and answered the call,
Then stepped out on solid ground
When others did fall.

Lord, help me to follow Your instructions too,
May I put You first in all I do!
Let me act on faith in You alone,
Then someday I'll meet Noah at Your throne.

Lost Now Found

God looks for us, then finds us,
And keeps us in His care.
He comes to seek & save the lost
And shows us He is there.

So hear God's voice, He's calling you –
You're forgiven of your sin.
He'll introduce you to His Love...
Once found, He'll work within.

Luke 19:10 – "The Son of Man came to seek & to save what was lost."

Giving For You

Help me focus more on You, Lord,
Thinking much less of myself,
Then as You give me blessings,
I'll give more to someone else.

Help me give up what I can
So my life for You I live –
Then trusting You with all I am,
I'll have more of my life to give.

What Are You Looking At?

If you look at the world & its problems,
You will be depressed.
If you look only at yourself,
You will become suppressed.
If you look at Jesus Christ,
You will be at rest.

Hebrews 12:2 – "Let us fix our eyes on Jesus, the author & perfecter of our faith..."

The Power of
Your Name

Many times we try to accomplish
All things on our own,
But then You remind me, Jesus,
To trust in You alone.

For I know it's not about the gifts
And goodness I accomplish,
But only by knowing Your mercy & grace,
I am totally astonished!

When I've done things for myself,
I truly was in vain,
But giving myself up for You, Jesus,
You work in the Power of Your Name.

The "SON"

Each morning there's a SON-rise
And it teaches me to say —
"God, I'll start my day reflecting
That You're here with me today."

He then starts showing me
How to serve & in what way —
And His SON-shine falls on me
To live His Love thru-out my day.

In the evening there's a SON-set
Where I rest in Him & say,
"Thank You for the moments
And how You lived thru me this day."

-Written 2-15-18

Be Mindful in Jesus

We hear nowadays "Be mindful",
Close your eyes. Watch how you breathe.
Do that yoga pose just right
And you can be stress-free.

But I have something better
That really works for me.
I keep my mind on Jesus Christ,
He loves & lives in me.

So I'll take my breath & focus my mind
On all He's done for me.
I'll say thank You for Your Love,
Your presence & Your peace.

And when I go thru-out my day,
I'll give my stress to Him.
He calms the storm, the wind & waves
As His Spirit works within.

GOOD ROOTS

Give my family GOOD ROOTS, Lord,
That grow only for You,
And let these roots grow down deep
So they know Your Word is true.

Be with them & let each know
You're with them here & now –
And grow faith deep in each heart, Lord,
Somewhere, someplace, somehow.

And then when all our time on earth
Is gone, complete & done –
In heaven we'll see our family
Together, souls blossomed in Your "Son."

Your Servant Beverly

My spiritual mentor was Beverly
Who taught in Christ you can be free –
When Satan brought my faith to kill,
She said, "God & I, we love you still."

I'll always remember her beautiful art,
Drawings by God – A visual start
To teach so many of the Risen King,
To her, her Savior was everything.

And as the years have flown quickly by,
With tears in my eyes, I start to cry,
'Thank You, God, for Your servant dear,
You knew thru Beverly, Your teachings I'd
hear.'

'A true example of Christian love,
A spiritual mother You sent from above,
Praise You! Two souls in heaven You'll see
'Cause I'll be there with Beverly.'

-Written 2-16-18

Wings of Hope

There's wings of hope He gives us
When we cannot seem to fly;
Remaining stagnant on the ground,
It seems as if we'll die.

But then the Spirit breathes in us
New hope, a gentle breeze –
Raising us up to fly again,
His strength lifts us with ease.

We cannot fly on our own,
Our hope will keep us down.
God's hope is sure & steadfast
To take us off the ground.

So look to His Hope & trust Him,
He's faithful & you'll see
With His Sure Hope, faith on your wings,
You'll fly high eternally.

Wings of Faith

God in His Wisdom chooses the way
For our faith to grow day by day -
Like a butterfly, emerging strong,
His Spirit uplifts & brings grace along.
First, we try to fill our life
With many other things,
Then Jesus comes along
And gives faith on 'Angel Wings'. —
To soar above the clouds
And see the SON so bright,
No longer in the dark
But in His amazing Light.

Serving You

Lord, make me available
In the life of someone today.
I accept Your invitation
To serve when & in what way.
For it is a gift, an honor
Called to serve with You;
No longer "master of my life,"
Savior, lead me in all I do.

-Written 2-21-18

Personal Guard

Lord, You say I should submit
Every thought to You,
And then the Mind of Christ
Will speak in all I say & do,
So Jesus, be the "personal guard"
Of my mind & heart,
Then when the door of my lips open,
Soft, loving words will start.

*Ps. 141:3 – "Set a guard over my mouth, O Lord;
keep watch over the door of my lips."*

A Coffee Break

Lord, help me fill my mind with You,
Then let Your Love fill my heart too.
Today I need a "pick me up"
And only You can "fill my cup."

Be Kind

Kindness makes a man attractive...
I read this in Proverbs today,
So today as I dress, I'll put kindness on –
Then, Lord, help me wear it all day!

Prov. 19:22 (TLB) – "Kindness makes a man attractive..."

Keep Me On Your Path

Keep me on Your path, Lord Jesus,
For You're the Life, the Truth, the Way,
So guide my steps by Your Word
As I go about my day.

For You know the plan You have for me
And all the moments in this day.
Let me live my life for You;
In Love's Truth & in Your Way.

Return & Repent

Return to me the Lord does say
And rend your heart to mine,
So I return myself to You,
O Giver of Love Divine.

Help me give, pray & fast for You,
In this season we call lent –
But most of all I'll remember You
Nailing my sins & repent.

*Joel 2:12 – "Even now," declares the Lord,
"return to me with all your heart,
with fasting & weeping & mourning."*

A Spring Poem

God, I want to grow in beauty & grace,
Only You can make that start,
So show me the seeds I should plant
In the "soil of my heart."

Spiritual Feast

I need a spiritual feast for all my needs,
I forget this & get tired.
You remind me, Lord, to drink from Your Well -
Your Word, renews my desire.

You encourage & lift my spirit again
As I retreat to You alone,
And feast my eyes only on You
And eat Words that come from Your Throne.

Forgive Me

Forgive me for putting myself first
And doing things my own way.
I need You, Lord of my life –
I surrender to You today!!

Grateful Thoughts & Good Attitudes

Our attitudes show
The way we look at things –
Like icy trees are "Ugh!"
Or we see diamonds sparkling!
And when the rain falls down,
I can sit in gloom,
Or know God's cleansing power
Washes me in the room.
And as the lightning cracks
And I hear the thunder roll –
Means there's music in God's Voice
And I know He's in control.
So, thank You, God, for grateful thoughts
That You can put in place –
For only You can turn a frown
Into a smile on my face!

-Written 3-7-18

Beauty of Jesus

Confess your sin & live by faith,
It's time to forget & move on.
Leave the blackness of sin & your disgrace —
Look to the Beauty of Jesus,
The beauty of grace…

Fruits of the Spirit

The fruits of the Spirit
Are hard to find —
And Jesus taught us to be loving & kind.
Now comes Jesus Christ
To work on my heart.
He gives fruits of the Spirit
And a brand new start.

-Written 3-16-18

Thank You

Dear God, thank You for blessing my life,
For comforting my heart with Your Love,
Thank You for strengthening my faith
With Your Holy Word from above.

Thank You for everything…
It's You that makes my heart sing!!

Redeemed

Jesus paid a price to set me free -
He bought me back from hell's misery.
He suffered for what He didn't deserve
And gave me paradise so my soul is preserved.

Be A Friend To All

When I think of friends I lost,
I wonder what's the reason?
Then Jesus says to love each one
He puts in every "season".

For as the years have marched & past,
God knows which friends to give us;
Some stay, some go, but all do come
Into our lives to teach us.

It's God who wants to change my heart;
Love, compassion & to give it –
Not just to the friends I want
But be a friend to all & live it.

To accept, not criticize, be kind
And care for people He brings my way,
To be a friend when someone needs
A "lift" or help today.

It's not about me choosing
Just certain friends to have –
But letting God choose friends for me
Brings the outcasts & the sad.

So here's the lesson I'm happy to say
I'm learning & I'll repeat –
I have more friends than ever today
By caring about each person God has me meet.

-Written 3-17-18

Water For My Soul

You are a mountain spring
And You're like a summer rain –
You drench my soul of thirst
And heal my heart of pain.

You are a raging sea
And a fresh-mist waterfall –
Thru storms I lean on You.
You refresh my heart & all.

You are a cleansing flood
And a well that never ends,
You remove my sins in Love –
Your life-giving water covers them.

Praise the Lord, then, O my soul –
Oh heart, give thanks & see;
Refreshed, renewed, restoring
Water poured on my soul for me.

Draw Near To God

When the devil comes to tempt you
To do things your own way,
If you give in...remember,
He steals your peace & joy today.

When the devil comes & says to you,
That's something you need to have...
Remember He kills relationships
And then everything goes bad.

When the devil comes & tells you,
Do life your way with me...
Remember He's there to destroy you;
You, your soul & your family.

Draw then near to God
And He'll draw near to you.
Grab His Hand to lead you,
In everything you do.

John 10:10 – "The thief comes only to steal,
& kill, & destroy;
I have come that they may have life,
& have it to the full."

Jesus - My Treasure

You teach me to set my heart on heaven
And to store up my treasures there –
For You are the only possession I need,
I need Your Love & care.
My love has grown so much for You –
I see Your goodness to me.
So now my treasures are service to You –
Built up in heaven for Thee.

*Matt. 6:19-20 – "Do not store up for yourselves
treasures on earth...
but store up for yourselves treasures in heaven."*

Eyes of Love

Jesus looks into our hearts
And sees with "eyes of love."
He sees the person we're meant to be
And transforms us from above.

Jesus looks into our hearts,
Loves us the way we are.
But the Spirit wants to live in us,
Shining His Bright & Morning Star.

Investing Time & Energy

How are you investing
Your energy today?
Worry is like a rocking chair...
It really goes nowhere.

So I'll invest my time
And energy in prayer –
I'll hand my worries "off to God",
Knowing He'll "take it from there."

Your Hand Of Might

Holy Spirit within me,
Your fingers lovingly mold
My heart & all I am
To be a servant bold. –
So help me speak the Truth,
Your Word, & walk in Light.-
For You're the Potter, I'm the clay
Shaped by Your Hand of Might.

Sharing Jesus

I've learned You don't just give me strength,
You are my strength when weak,
For You redeemed this stubborn clay
With power so I would speak
Of Jesus' Love, His life for mine,
His Love for their lives too.
With courage now You send me out
To share Jesus in all I do.

His Life For Mine

He gave His life for me...
So I would give my life for Him.
His life was nailed with love for me
To save my soul from sin.

He rose with power for me –
My death He now was given,
He saved my soul to rise again
And live with Him in heaven.

This Place Of Grace

Lord, thank You for Your beauty & grace,
You bless our lives in this place.

May all who come be blessed within,
To know Your Love forgives their sin.

Let us serve & freely share
With our neighbors Your Love & care.

Listen!

Take time to listen to the Voice of God,
He speaks His Word to you –
So listen to the gospel preached,
'Cause God tells you what to do.

So don't just sit in church this week,
Listen with your heart –
What's one thing God is telling you?
Then go & do your part.

This past Sunday I wrote this down;
God spoke to me this way:
'Use God's Word as your guide,
And live in His wisdom of faith'.

Dreams Come True

You hold dreams for me to do,
Help with plans working for You.
Here is my heart for You to fill,
Give me steps to do Your Will.

Gone are Satan's holds on me,
Won by grace & victory…
Your Son died to set me free,
Salvation's come…I can be "me".

New creation…All things new!
Now there is Your work to do!
Redeemer, Spirit, Teacher, Friend,
You'll do the work, You say "begin"!

Thanks & praise, Your Majesty!
Your Beauty, order is in me –
To use what talents I can bring,
You make my life an offering.

Honor, glory to Your Name!
You live! I'll never be the same.
You washed me clean & I'm made new!
Now with my Savior, "dreams come true".

-Written 2-9-17

Your Way of Life

Without You, Jesus, we know we would
Destroy ourselves, it's true –
We'd live in a lonely 'prison of sin',
Soul-crushing desires & selfish living too.

We know we would self-destruct
With bad habits & lifestyle –
But You came with Loving grace
To make our lives worthwhile.

We know Your Way of living
Is life-giving, peaceful too –
You put us on a path of freedom
And make us new creations too.

Thank You for choosing us in Love,
For we could never choose You.
Thank You for saving us from ourselves,
The world & the devil too.

Praise be to You, the Lord of Life!
Praise You for setting us free –
To live for You, on Your path for us,
Where You teach us who to be.

John 15:16 – " You did not choose me, but I chose you..."

Jer. 29:11 – "For I know the plans I have for you," declares the Lord, "plans to prosper you & not to harm you, plans to give you hope & a future."

Dream With God

My soul will rejoice & I will dream
Made in the image of God.
For God only sees what your dream will be
And sees things that are not.

Dreams make the difference between living a
life,
And living a life for God —
So I will sit in the presence of God
And find a quiet spot.

I'll thank the Lord for my talents & treasures
That He gave me years ago —
And ask how to serve Him with these gifts
That I am blessed to know.

I'll thank the Lord for the faith given me
And all He's done so far —
Considering what isn't & what could be,
His Spirit takes us beyond what we are.

So plant me where You want me, Lord,
Bloom & grow my spirit —
With You all things are possible,
Dream a "dream for my life"… Help me live it.

Move Forward
In The New

Forget what's in the past!
I'll move forward in the new –
God, plant & bloom Your dreams for me...
I surrender myself to You.

Teach me only to think of You,
Also, others as I should –
I know You make all things work out,
You work all things for Your good.

So I give You all my cares & thoughts,
And leave it up to You.
Bring Your Beauty in my life, dear Lord,
In all I am & do.

Hospitality

Hospitality seems to be lost these days
Trying to have perfect homes & perfect ways –
But God has shown me His beauty & grace
Can live anywhere & in any place.

So today I'll keep Him in mind –
Invite someone in & just be kind.
Lord, show me who & show me when,
It's a welcoming space, so let's begin!

Hospitality is about connection,
Not a home that is in perfection!
Just speak kind words & a listening ear,
And let all know that Christ lives here!

Give Him Thanks

Thank You, Lord, for all good gifts
You give thru-out my life —
Blessings, abundance, too numerous to count,
Always there amidst the strife.

So today let me focus on all good things
And list blessings You've given me.
I'll pause & think of the goodness of You —
Then give thanks on bended knee.

*Ps. 107:1 – "Give thanks to the Lord, for He is
good;
His love endures forever."*

The Christmas Call

Merry Christmas, one and all!
Have you heard the Christmas call?
Yes! I put up Christmas lights.
My tree is done. It looks just right!

Merry Christmas, one and all!
Have you heard the Christmas call?
Yes! I started shopping now!
Those stores are busy in the mall.

Merry Christmas, one and all!
Have you heard the Christmas call?
Yes! The house is decorated, stockings hung,
I almost have my baking done.

Merry Christmas, one and all!
Have you heard the Christmas call?
Our family's get-together is always great!
We finally got a "nailed-down" date!

Merry Christmas, one and all!
I just heard the Savior's call.
This call so meek, a call so mild,
The faint cry of a little child.

It's hard to hear with all the noise!
It's hard to see Him thru the toys!
God sent a baby in a barn-yard stall,
And He waits for us to hear the call.

God is calling one and all,
To see His Love in a baby small.
This Love comes down for you and me
To rescue us for eternity.

Continued

101

Many years ago God said,
He'd send a Savior in a manger bed.
He comes each year in this quiet way,
And calls our heart to believe today.

This baby is a gift of Love –
Born for you from up above –
He came and died, then rose you know,
This was all to save your soul.

We're dead in sin and cannot face
Him in heaven, a perfect place.
Hear the call! A baby cries!
For you He comes on earth to die.

He died to take your sins away
And conquers death for you today,
So put down all your Christmas lists,
Listen, see, take notice of this!

This baby died and rose as King!
It's why you hear the angels sing!
Be wise then, like the men who searched,
They knelt and worshipped at His birth.

Years have past since the star shone bright-
Why do we hang those Christmas lights?
The Light of the World still comes today,
To save you from going your own, wrong way.

Jesus is the Truth and Light,
And just for you He comes this night.
Merry Christmas, one and all!
Stop! And hear God's Christmas call!

By Karen Lueders
11-29-17
To God Be The Glory!

His Gift For You

This Christmas I'm thinking
Of the Magi three,
Who searched & worshipped
On bended knee.
They bowed before Jesus
And gave Him their treasures –
This baby...A king!
Time & distance couldn't measure.

Three gifts they gave Him
And what did He do?
He gave three gifts back
To them, me & you!
Thirty years from His birth,
He died on a cross,
Rose victorious & ascended –
His gifts for the lost!

Now reigning as King
On heaven's high throne –
Looking down on His children,
He calls them His own.
Hmm...What gift can I give Him
This Christmas to start?
I know! I will give Him
The gift of my heart.

Continued

103

But wait! Another gift He
Wants us to receive?
Yes! He gives the Gift of Salvation
To a heart that believes.
So be a wise man today,
Search & see –
There's a gift with your name
Under "His tree" –

Perfectly wrapped, now open His call,
For you: The gift is heaven!
From: The Savior of all!

By Karen Lueders
11-27-18
To God Be The Glory!

Daily Prayers...
Life's Lessons...
Daily Thoughts...

A Daily Prayer
Lord, I cannot do things on my own
So be my strength & help alone.

A Daily Prayer
Lord, forgive my many sins
And wash me up completely –
Help purify my thoughts, words, deeds,
With the fresh start You now give me.

I John 1:9 – "If we confess our sins,
He is faithful & just
& will forgive us our sins & purify us from all
unrighteousness."

A Daily Prayer
Be my words & thoughts today
In all I say & do,
May Your Love live inside my heart
To honor & serve You.

A Daily Prayer
When I stumble, when I sin...
Take me back to start again!

A Daily Prayer
I'm created by God,
Redeemed by Christ,
And empowered by the Spirit-
So use me as You will, dear Lord,
And truly help me live it.

A Daily Prayer
I offer myself to You today-
Use me in Your Will & Way.
Let me share Your Love with all,
Give me wisdom to hear Your call.

A Daily Prayer
Refresh my heart,
Revive my heart,
With You there is
A brand new start.
Teach me to number all my days
And live Your Love in a whole new way.

A Daily Prayer
God, You say to be humble
And only be kind...
Help me do this today, Lord,
Keeping You in my mind.

A Daily Prayer
Lord, let Your Word enter
My heart, mind & spirit –
And then with Your strength, Lord,
Help me truly live it!

*Deut. 6:5 – "Love the Lord Your God with all
your heart
& with all your soul & with all your strength."*

A Daily Prayer
Before I rush to start my day,
Remind me, Lord, to kneel & pray.
Telling You all my cares,
Your peace will take me anywhere.

A Daily Prayer
Lord, bless me with inner grace & beauty –
When people see the kindness done,
Lord, ONLY let them see Your SON.

A Daily Prayer
Lord, use me however You choose
In the life of someone today.
Make me available to serve You
Wherever & in whatever way.

A Daily Prayer
You are so amazing, Lord,
And how You work in me,
But the most amazing thing is that
Your forgiving Love has saved me!

A Daily Prayer
God, You say You'll meet my needs,
And I think only of my wants,
So teach me to live simply,
Thanking You for what I've got!!

Phil. 4:19 – "And my God will meet all your needs according to His glorious riches in Christ Jesus."

A Daily Prayer
One day follows another
In this world of trouble & pain.
Evil is with us & all around
As the devil tries to reign.
Remind me, Lord, You're still in charge,
Help me remember this as I should,
And by Your Almighty Power,
You work all things for Your good.

A Daily Prayer
Lord, thank You for loving me
Enough to break me
'Cause only then can You
Remake me.

A Daily Prayer
Father, fulfill Your purposes for me
And help to give myself generously.

A Daily Prayer
Help me with my day
And teach me how to pray.
What should I do to love & serve You?
When resistance sets in –
Teach me to begin!
Guide my day only in Your Way.

A Daily Prayer
Come, Holy Spirit,
Work in my heart.
Renew my spirit
With a fresh, new start.

A Daily Prayer
Cleanse me, refresh me –
Make me new!
Do this, Lord…
Let me only serve You!!

A Daily Prayer
Lord, make me truly humble,
I can't but know You can -
Teach me to be Your servant
Led by Your Mighty Hand.

I Peter 5:6 – "Humble yourselves, therefore,
under God's mighty Hand,
that He may lift you up in due time."

A Daily Prayer
Lord, help me not to strive
In everything I do –
I'll give You all my tasks
And You'll gently see me thru.

A Daily Prayer
I rely on You & trust You, Lord,
My worries I'll cast aside.
I know You're in control of all,
So I'll keep Your peace in mind.

A Daily Prayer
Whatever you are going thru,
There's always hope when skies are blue,
And when you think you're at your end,
God says, "There's hope – Let's start again!"

A Daily Prayer
God, I take so much for granted,
Many times thinking only of me –
So I'll stop & think of my blessings;
Your care & love for me.

A Daily Prayer
Like a tea kettle with a spout,
Pour me over & tip love out!

A Daily Prayer
Today's a new day,
Help me live by Your Word –
So guide me to follow
Your direction, Lord.

A Daily Prayer
Help me, Father, make the most
Of every day I have,
For each new day's a gift from You
So I'll make someone glad.

A Daily Prayer
Lord, You teach me to forget
And leave my sin behind –
Then go & help someone for You.
Be thankful, gentle, kind.

A Daily Prayer
Teach me how to change my life
In thought, in Word & deed.
You're the Potter, I'm the clay
So, Father, work in me.

A Daily Prayer
You're in control & I want to be,
So take this worry away from me.
I lift my arms way in the air,
"You're in control! I'll leave it there!"

A Daily Prayer
God, help prayer be "part of me",
So I'll give You my hurts naturally.
'Cause why should I hold on to them
When You will take every single one?
"Peace! Peace! You say, just come to me.
Your hurts I'll take, now glorify me."

A Daily Prayer
Give hurts to God & say, "forgive me";
Then glorify God thankfully.

Daily Prayer
Father, clean my heart, thoughts, spirit I
pray,
Let Jesus shine brightly in me today!

A Daily Prayer
You answer my prayer
When I give You each care –
You show me in love
That You're watching above.

A Daily Prayer
Keep me on Your path, Lord Jesus;
You're the Life, the Truth, the Way –
And guide my steps by Your Word
As I go about my day.

*Ps. 119:105 – "Your Word is a lamp to my feet
& a light for my path."*

A Daily Prayer
When I pray, You're always near,
Thank You, Lord, for being here!

*Is. 58:9 – "Then you will call, & the Lord
will answer;
you will cry for help, & He will say:
Here am I."*

A Daily Prayer
I'll cast my care on You, Lord,
Now in the morning hour –
Then take the gift of Your peace,
Strength, joy, wisdom, power.

A Daily Prayer
Lord, for each & every situation
I cannot recall –
I pray Your help & healing,
Great Physician, over all.

Life's Lesson
Who should I help?
What should I do?
Today's a new day...
Help me only serve You.

For time marches on...
Years of serving myself-
I'm giving my life now
To serve someone else.

Life's Lesson
I have found success to be...
Having the 'GREAT I AM' over me;
To follow His Ways & do what's right,
He blesses your life with His Mighty Light.

Life's Lesson
Greatest joys & deep despair
I have seen in life,
But faithfully, He remains the same
He's with you thru each strife.

"Be Still My Soul" – Based on the hymn
'Be Still My Soul' vs. 1
"Leave to Thy God to order & provide. In every
change He faithfully will remain."

Life's Lesson
The "what-ifs" of life
Can choke-out faith
And deaden me to pray.-
So when I worry, I'll hand cares to You.
You're in-charge anyway.

Life's Lesson
Satan had asked to sift me like wheat –
Then Jesus prayed for me,
Now I kneel at Jesus' feet.

Luke 22:31 – "...Satan has asked to sift you
like wheat.
But I have prayed for you...that your faith may
not fail."

Life's Lesson
"Don't take it personally" we say
When remarks hurt you & I.
We think about it, stew & sulk,
We even might just cry.

But wait! Jesus comes with promises
And says, "Personally take *these* to heart;
Joy, peace, rest, strength & love –
Help & comfort I impart."

Life's Lesson
Stuff is "stuff",
There's never enough –
I've learned in time,
Keep people in mind.

Stuff takes time & energy,
I'm content making a happy memory!

Life's Lesson
What's the secret of being content,
The pursuit of happiness in life?
Well, I've learned the secret's in my soul
And the answer is in Christ.

Life's Lesson
Truth is always the right choice,
Make truth always your goal.
Lies are too easy to "trip over"-
And lies will rot your soul.

Ps. 86:11a – "Teach me Your Way, O Lord, and I will walk in Your Truth..."

Life's Lesson
Don't be selfish & try to impress!
Be humble, think others better than yourself.

Phil. 2:3 – "Do nothing out of selfish ambition or vain conceit, but in humility consider others better than yourselves."

Life's Lesson
Always be full of joy in the Lord.
I say it again, "Rejoice!"
Don't let the devil bring "doom & gloom"
When the Savior is your choice!

Phil. 4:4 – "Rejoice in the Lord always. I will say it again: Rejoice!"
Jude vs. 24 – "To Him who is able to keep you from falling & to present you before His glorious presence without fault & with great joy – to the only God our Savior be glory, majesty, power & authority, thru Jesus Christ our Lord, before all ages, now & forevermore! Amen."

Life's Lesson
Delight in the day & don't lose your way
Looking back on past mistakes –
Press on toward the goal, God's prize for your
soul,
God calls you heavenward, for Jesus' sake.

*Phil. 3:13 -14 "...Forgetting what is behind &
straining toward what is ahead,
I press on toward the goal to win the prize
for which God called me heavenward in Christ
Jesus."*

Life's Lesson
Today You remind me to forget the past
And also forget the good –
For past achievements mean nothing now...
Today! Help me be & do what I should!

Life's Lesson
You must become greater,
I must become less.
Your grace & Your power
Is made perfect in weakness.

*John 3:30 – "He must become greater; I must
become less."
II Cor. 12:9 – But He said to me, "My grace is
sufficient for you,
for my power is made perfect in weakness."*

Life's Lesson
Life is all about loving God,
Then loving others too –
It really is as simple as that;
God first, then others, then you.

Life's Lesson
Joy, generosity, beauty & grace –
Humility learned, let me serve in this place.

Life's Lesson
It's never a decision we've made
When we come to know Jesus Christ.
It's only by the Grace of God,
He comes to change my life.

It's not about giving my heart to Him,
But His heart loving mine.
His perfect love is given for me
And I'm His…O, Love Divine!

My Friend
When I think of blessings,
It's you that comes to mind,
You've been with me thru "thick & thin"-
A truer friend I'll never find.

A Daily Thought
Put beauty first as you start your day,
Thinking only of God above;
Then go & scatter kindness around
Giving "little bouquets" of His Love!

A Daily Thought
Have you given anything lately to truly see,
God can help others thru your generosity?

A Daily Thought
Pride gets in the way of "us" –
Remember this: IN GOD WE TRUST.
Stop trying to do things your own way,
TRUST IN GOD to lead the way.

A Daily Thought
There's many things to complain about,
To be discouraged & cause me doubt,
But I will thank & praise the One
Who gives strength & wisdom to overcome.

*Phil. 2:14 – "Do everything without
complaining or arguing..."*

A Daily Thought
When everything in life
Seems coming to an end,
God takes our hand & "lifts us up"-
Saying, "Let's begin again."

A Daily Thought
Let's be quiet & trust in God
And then we'll know He's there,
To help us with each trial we face,
And know we're in His care.

A Daily Thought
Lord, Your promising sunrise shows
Your mercies never cease,
And sunsets promise me sweet sleep
Where my soul rests in Your peace.

A Daily Thought
The blackness of sin or the Beauty of Grace –
It's a choice that we live in!
So I thank the Lord for His mercy & love –
Darkness behind! Beauty lives in its place...

A Daily Thought
God commands that we be strong,
Courageous not afraid.
We need not be discouraged
'Cause He's with us every day.

Joshua 1:9 – "Have I not commanded you? Be strong & courageous. Do not be terrified; do not be discouraged, for the Lord your God will be with you wherever you go."

<u>A Daily Thought</u>
Be full of joy & generosity!
Asking God to do His part –
Then all will know You belong to God,
It shows! He's in your heart.

<u>A Daily Thought</u>
THANK the Lord as you start your day,
THANK the Lord before going your way!
PRAISE the Lord in the heavens above,
PRAISE the Lord for His might & love.

Ps. 100:4b - "Give thanks to Him & praise His Name."

<u>A Daily Thought</u>
Look at all your blessings!
Thank the Lord & then,
Pass them on to someone else,
A stranger or a friend.

<u>A Daily Thought</u>
Be strong today in the Lord,
Each & every hour –
So when the devil attacks you,
He will have no power.

Eph. 6:10 – "Be strong in the Lord & in His mighty power..."

A Daily Thought
You paid the price to set me free.
You died in love to live in me.

A Daily Thought
I was so beaten down,
Then You picked me up,
And overflowed blessings
Into my empty cup.

A Daily Thought
Linger in the presence of Jesus today
So you go out in joy & serve in His Way.

A Daily Thought
I cannot hear You when I doubt,
Criticize others or when I pout –
Today I'll listen for Your "whispers of love",
And follow Your direction from above.

A Daily Thought
Today I'll choose Your Light & Love –
Darkness is gone in Christ above.

A Daily Thought
The devil is the "undertaker",
He puts you down all the time –
But Jesus is the "Overtaker",
He "lifts" you up to joy sublime.

A Daily Thought

When past sin comes to mind,
Acknowledge God's forgiveness in His Son —
Then thank the Lord for His promise of Love,
Forget your past...Move on!!!

Isaiah 43:25 – "I, even I, am He who blots out
your transgressions, for my own sake,
& remembers your sins no more."

To Your Glory

Everything I am & everything I do,
Is empowered with Your Love
And given back to You.

To God Be The Glory!
Karen R. Lueders

THANK YOU!

Thank You God for singing
Songs over me at night —
And giving me the poetry
In the early morning light.

Ps. 42:8 – "By day the Lord directs His Love,
at night His song is with me —
a prayer to the God of my life."

Contact
Karen Lueders
at
karenlueders@yahoo.com

to purchase books and/or poetry
and music presentations.

Made in the USA
Middletown, DE
12 August 2019